CN01640761

# Gases

## Contents



## About this unit

This unit introduces children to gases. They begin by thinking about air and learn that, even though it is not visible, air is all around them. Children learn that gases, like liquids and solids, are a form of material and that gases can be made when liquids evaporate. Children compare the behaviour of gases with that of solids and liquids, in terms of keeping shape and volume, and ease of flow.

**Scientific enquiry** is planned into the unit and focuses on:

- making careful observations and measurements.
- investigating the properties of gases through simple experimentation.
- applying knowledge gained from observations and enquiries.

# Background Scientific Information

## What is a gas?

Most materials can change to any one of three forms – solid, liquid or gas. A gas is simply one form of a material. Most of the materials we think of as gases, such as oxygen or nitrogen, are gases at the temperatures we experience in our normal everyday life. However, if you make gases very cold they will change into liquids. Make them colder still and they turn into solids. For example, oxygen changes from a gas into a liquid at around -183°C; and liquid oxygen changes into solid oxygen at around -219°C. Similarly, materials that are solid at everyday temperatures can change into liquids and then gases as we make them hotter. For example, solid iron changes into liquid iron at 1535°C, and liquid iron changes into gaseous iron at 2750°C.

Some everyday substances, such as mist, foam, bubbles and spray, are mixtures of liquids and gases. Because gases are often not visible, we tend to think that they will have little or no weight. In fact they may weigh more than we think. If you imagine trying to pick up a suitcase that had all the air from a classroom squashed into it, you would find that it weighed a considerable amount.

## What is air?

Air is a mixture of gases. Ask most people to tell you the main gas in the air, and they will reply that it is oxygen. They can be quite surprised to find that nitrogen is the main constituent of air making up about 78% of it. Oxygen is only about 21% of the air. Argon is the third most common gas in the air at 0·09% and carbon dioxide is next at 0·03%.

## What are the differences in the behaviour of solids, liquids and gases?

There are two ways to think about the differences between solids, liquids and gases. We can either think about the arrangement and movement of particles or we can think about the way gases, liquids and solids behave in terms of their gross features – in other words, how a lump of it would behave. In this unit, children compare the behaviour of gases, solids and liquids in the latter way, as shown on this table.

| | Solid | Liquid | Gas |
|---|---|---|---|
| Does it keep its shape? | Yes | No | No |
| Does it keep its volume? | Yes | Yes | No |
| Does it flow? | No | Yes | Yes |

## Which gases do we use in everyday life?

We use a large number of gases for many different purposes. For example, carbon dioxide is used in fire extinguishers and for carbonated drinks; nitrous oxide for anaesthetics; hydrogen for rocket fuel and the manufacture of margarine; helium for welding and in balloons; nitrogen in food packaging and pipeline purging; oxygen for making steel, treating waste water and supporting life; and argon for filling light bulbs and fluorescent tubes. Our modern lifestyle would be difficult to maintain if we were unable to make and use these and other gases.

## Water

Water is a unique material. It exists on Earth in all three states of matter - solid, liquid and gas - within a narrow temperature band. Below 0°C it is a solid - ice. Between 0°C and 100°C it is a liquid, and above 100°C it is an invisible gas. Most water that exists in the air, as steam, mist, fog or clouds, however, forms below 100°C and is technically known as water vapour rather than water gas. Water vapour consists of tiny droplets of water dispersed through the air and this is what we commonly call 'steam'. True steam is water gas and is invisible; this is the gas that is in the clear first inch or so at the spout of a boiling kettle, for example . At this stage children are not required to distinguish between water vapour and gas, and in this unit these two terms are interchangeable.

# Information and Communication Technology

Where appropriate, ideas for ICT opportunities are included throughout the Teacher's Notes. The table below indicates where ICT skills could be developed in this unit.

| Task | | ICT Opportunity |
|---|---|---|
| 3 | Spot the gases | *Word process a list. Use database software.* |
| 8 | What is air? | *Use database and graphing software to make a chart.* |
| 9 | How heavy is fizz? | *Use a digital camera and a word processor or desktop publishing software.* |
| 10 | Gas is handy stuff. | *Research using CD-ROMs and the Internet.* |

# Scheme of Work:

| Learning objective: Knowledge and understanding | Task | Learning objective: Skills | Literacy and numeracy links | Resources and safety | Evidence of learning Children: |
|---|---|---|---|---|---|
| There are differences between solids and liquids. | **1 Sorting solids and liquids.** Children revise what they know about solids and liquids. | | | | Can sort materials into solids and liquids. Can describe features of solids and liquids. Can recognise that temperature affects the state of a material. |
| | **2 What do you know about gases?** Children offer their initial ideas about gases and ask questions about gases. **3 Spot the gases.** Children find out whether they know the names of any gases depicted in a picture. | Ask scientific questions. | | **Task Sheets 1, 2.** Word processor. | Can discuss ideas about gases. Can ask questions about gases. |
| Air has weight and is all around us. | **4 Where's the air?** Children carry out a number of quick activities which provide evidence that air exists. **5 Persuading Paul.** Children write a letter and construct an argument to persuade someone that air is real. | Use evidence to explain. | Write a letter. Construct an argument. | Sponge, water, bowl, large piece of card, paper, glass or beaker, beads in jar, full balloon, empty balloon, digital balance measuring to 0·1g. | Can refer to the effect of the presence of air in the various activities. Can construct an argument for the existence of air. |
| Solid materials have air in the 'gaps'. | **6 How much air is in gravel?** Children pour water onto gravel to find out how much air it replaced. They consider why others in the class have got different results and why they should take repeat readings. | Know how and why to take repeat readings. | Measure volume. Calculate volume of air by finding the difference between two readings. | Fine gravel, $100cm^3$ measuring cylinders, water. **Safety!** Make sure that children wear plastic gloves to handle gravel. | Know that water replaces air in the gravel. Can suggest why different people have different results and why they should take repeat readings. Can use a middle value from repeat readings. |
| Soils have air trapped in them. | **7 How much air is in different soils.** Children carry out a fair test, taking repeat readings to find out how much air is in different soils. | Measure the volume of water carefully. Decide how important it is to take repeat readings. Explain how we know that some soils have more air than others. | Obtain information from non-fiction text. | **Task Sheets 3, 4.** Different soils, $100cm^3$ measuring cylinders, water. **Safety!** Make sure that children wear plastic gloves to handle soils. | Can set up and carry out a fair test safely. Can measure volume carefully. Can say why it is important to take repeat readings. Can refer to evidence to compare the amount of air in different soils. |
| There are many gases and many of these are important to us. | **8 What is air?** Children consider how much of each gas is in air. | | Construct a chart. | Database and graphing software. | Know that nitrogen is the most common gas in air, there is some oxygen and very small amounts of argon and carbon dioxide. Can draw a chart of the different gases in the air. |
| Gases have weight. | **9 How heavy is fizz?** Children discuss what might happen when they compare the weight of an unopened can of fizzy drink and an opened can that has gone flat. They write a newspaper report of their findings. | | Write a newspaper report using a computer to prepare and design it. | **Task Sheet 5.** Cans of fizzy drink, digital scales or pan balance. Word processor. Digital camera. | Know that a can containing flat pop weighs less than an unopened can because gases have weight. |

| Learning objective: Knowledge and understanding | Task | Learning objective: Skills | Literacy and numeracy links | Resources and safety | Evidence of learning Children: |
|---|---|---|---|---|---|
| | **10 Gas is handy stuff.** Children research information about different gases and how we use them in everyday life. They make an interactive display of their information. | | Locate and present information to others. | Reference books, CD-ROMs, Internet. | Know about several different gases and their uses from their own and others' research. |
| Gases are formed when liquids evaporate. | **11 Where do gases come from?** Children consider what has happened to water that has evaporated.<br>**12 The perfume particle's journey.** Children write a story or create a drama, telling how a particle of perfume travels from a dish to someone's nose. | | Plan and write a narrative story. | Tank of water with level marked on the side. Small amount of liquid perfume (not spray). | Know that the water and perfume changed from liquid to gas and that they evaporated. |
| Gases flow easily. | **13 What do gases do?** Children complete a table to show what they know about solids and liquids. Children consider how gases behave in comparison to solids and liquids. They suggest ways to test their ideas.<br>**14 How much gas is in a bottle of pop?** Children see how much gas comes from a bottle of pop. They set up a fair test and identify possible causes of inaccuracies in their results. They decide how much to trust their results. | Decide how to answer a question. Set up a fair test Identify how much to trust results | | **Task Sheets 6, 7, 8.** Syringes, balloons, bottles of pop, rubber bung, tube, screw clip or a 'Hoffman' clip, 3 or 4 litre measuring cylinders filled with water, large plastic bowl, beehive stand or similar.<br>**Safety!** Always be careful to make sure syringes do not have needles in them and remind the children not to play with them outside school. | Can describe how they know that gases do not keep their shape or volume and flow easily.<br>Know that squashed (compressed) gas is put in fizzy drinks and that the volume expands when the bottle is opened.<br>Can set up a fair test to answer a question. Can identify that some gas may have escaped, and that some may still remain in the liquid and that results cannot be trusted completely. |
| | **Checkpoint.** Children amend text about gases and make suggestions. | | Edit text. | **Task Sheet 9.** | |
| | **Summary.** Children read through the statements and complete the **Science Log**. | | | **Science Log.** | |
| | **Assessment Tasks.** Children do structured tests to assess their knowledge and understanding of gases. | | | **Assessment Task Sheets A and B.** | |
| | | | | | |

## TASK 1 What do you know about solids and liquids?

### Purpose

To revise children's knowledge of solids and liquids.

### What to do

The main purpose of this activity is to encourage the children to recall what they know about solids and liquids before beginning work on gases. Sorting the different materials shown in the pictures into solids and liquids should be fairly straightforward. Allow the children time to discuss the sentences about solids and liquids in groups or pairs, to help them recall previous work. Look at page 3 to remind them that liquids can change into solids when cooled, and solids can change into liquids when heated. They should recognise that whether a material is solid or liquid depends on its temperature. Remind them that when we refer to a material as a solid or a liquid, we are really saying that at normal everyday temperatures a material is solid or liquid.

| QUESTIONS | *Possible answers* |
|---|---|
| • Which of these are solids? | *Foil, wax and ice.* |
| • Which of these are liquids? | *Water, vinegar and oil.* |
| • What can we say about solids? | *They do not flow – they keep their shape.* |
| • What can we say about solids and liquids? | *They keep their volume.* |
| • What can we say about liquids? | *They flow, they make a level surface, they take the shape of their container and they change shape.* |
| • How does a solid change into a liquid? | *When it gets hotter it melts.* |
| • How does a liquid change into a solid? | *When it gets colder it freezes, or solidifies.* |
| • Can we say that a material will always be a solid or a liquid? | *No. It depends on the temperature.* |

## TASK 2 What do you know about gases?

### Purpose

For children to offer their ideas about gases and how to tell whether a material is a gas and for them to ask questions to trigger ideas.

### What to do

Ask them to discuss the statements about gases. Explain that at this point you simply want to know what ideas they have and to help them identify things they might want to find out about gases. You do not expect them to know all the answers. Ask them to write their ideas on **Task Sheet 1**.

Collect together everyone's thoughts about gases, and bring out the main features, for example 'most of us think all gases explode when you put a match near them but some of us aren't sure whether that's true'. Do not be tempted to tell them the answers at this stage. Give the children a time limit and ask them to work in pairs to write down a question about gases to which they would like the answer. Find some way to display their questions, such as making a question display board, or a question mobile. Some questions will probably be answered as they work their way through the unit. Other questions you can offer as a challenge for others to answer by using their research skills for homework. Add their answers to the display and put a date when the class was able to answer each question. The display can then provide a record of the progress of the class.

### Watch out for!

Many children have difficulty discussing and thinking about gases because they are usually invisible. Reassure them that it is all right to say that gases are hard to think about.

TASK 3

## Spot the gases

**Purpose**

For children to describe all the different types of gases they know about.

**What to do**

Ask the children to look at the picture and, on **Task Sheet 2**, circle the places where they would expect to find a gas or gases. Ask them to give you the names of any gases. Once again, point out that they are not expected to know the answers but that you want to find out what they already know. Make a note of the names of gases that the majority of the children do and don't know.

**QUESTIONS**

- What is in the balloons?
- Which gas is used in the barbecue?
- What makes pop fizzy?
- What gas is in the car tyres? And the paddling pool?
- Where else can you see gases being used?

**ICT OPPORTUNITY**

Children could word process their list and make a class database of their answers at this stage. They could add to the database as they learn more about what different gases are used for.

**Watch out for!**

Children may not know the names of any gases other than air. Reassure them that this is fine at this stage of the unit.

TASK 4

## Where's the air?

**Purpose**

For children to know that air is all around us and has weight.

**What to do**

Set up the activities as shown in the **Pupil's Book**. Either allow the children to try out these things for themselves by setting up a circus of activities or, if there is limited space and a large number of children, carry out the activities as demonstrations asking children, particularly those who might need convincing that air exists, to help you. Ask questions about each activity. If running this session as a circus, write the questions on cards and place them beside each activity.

| QUESTIONS | *Possible answers* |
|---|---|
| What is in the bubbles that come out of the sponge when you squeeze it under water? | *Air.* |
| Why is it hard to run when you are holding a large piece of card? | *The air pushes back on the card.* |
| Why doesn't the paper in the bottom of the inverted glass get wet when you put it in a bowl of water? | *There is air inside the glass. This stops the water from getting inside the glass.* |
| When your pour water onto beads (or marbles) in a jar, why do you get bubbles? | *There is air between the beads (or marbles) and this makes air bubbles.* |
| Why does a balloon full of air weigh more than an empty balloon? | *Air is real stuff. Even though we can't see it, it has weight.* |

## TASK 5 Persuading Paul

**Purpose**

For children to explain that we can use evidence to show that air is real.

**What to do**

Let the children read Paul's letter. Ask them to discuss what evidence they could use to convince Paul that air exists even though it is not visible. Suggest they make notes about what they want to say. Point out the sentence starters given at the bottom of the page and suggest that they might like to include some of these in their reply to Paul.

| QUESTIONS | *Possible answers* |
| --- | --- |
| • Why does Paul think that air does not exist? | *Because it is invisible.* |
| • What evidence is there that air exists? | |

## TASK 6 How much air is in gravel?

**Purpose**

For children to know that gravel has air between the stones and to know how and why to take repeat readings.

**What to do**

Collect enough fine gravel to provide enough for pairs, or small groups of children, to put 50cm$^3$ in a measuring cylinder. Ask them to carry out the task as shown and to calculate the amount of air that was in their gravel. Take in the results from all the groups. Inevitably, there will be some variation. Ask them to offer reasons for the variation in results and suggest they refer to their notes about which parts were difficult to carry out accurately. Ask them to decide which result is most likely to be a typical result. They should go for the answer in the middle of the spread of values or choose the mode or most common result. Point out that scientists often find they get slightly different readings when they repeat them because it is impossible to carry things out in the same way and to measure exactly the same value each time. In repeating their readings they have a chance of getting closer to a typical value and increasing accuracy.

| QUESTIONS | *Possible answers* |
| --- | --- |
| • Which parts were hard to measure accurately? Why? | *It was hard to measure 50cm$^3$ of gravel accurately because some bits stuck up above the line and some were below.* |
| • Why have we got different results? | *There are many points where we could have carried things out slightly differently, such as putting in different amounts of gravel; not using gravel with identical lumps of stone; getting different readings in parts that were hard to measure accurately.* |
| • Which of your readings do you think is most likely to be near the answer? | *The answer will depend on results but we should select a reading that is the middle of the spread of results.* |

**Watch out for!**

**Safety!** Make sure that children wear plastic gloves to handle gravel and that they wash their hands afterwards.

TASK 7

# How much air is in different soils?

## Purpose

For children to know that soils have air trapped in them and for them to measure the volume of water carefully, decidc how important it is to take repeat readings and to explain how we know that some soils have more air than others.

## What to do

Collect together the equipment needed and spread newspaper, or another covering, on the table where the soils will be handled. Try to include soils that are distinctly different from each other such as sand, peat and clay. You will need reasonably large amounts of soil as groups of children will be repeating their readings. At this stage, the children should be able to carry out this investigation with a reasonable degree of independence. Leave them to complete the planning board using **Task Sheet 3**. Point out that, following the previous activity with gravel, you will be particularly interested to see how important they think it will be to take repeat readings in this investigation and to see the reasons they give. Offer support where needed by asking questions such as those below. Once groups have had their plans checked by you, ask them to carry out the enquiry and complete the table and bar chart on **Task Sheet 4**. Ask them to predict how much air would be in a mixture of two equal amounts of their soils, for example, sand and peat. Encourage them to refer to their bar chart to make this prediction. Allow them to try it out and to see how close they were to the answer. Bring the class together to talk about what different groups found out and, finally, ask them to consider who might want to have information about the amount of air in different soils.

| QUESTIONS | *Possible answers* |
|---|---|
| • What are you changing? | *The type of soil.* |
| • What are you measuring? | *The volume of air in the soil.* |
| • How can you make sure that it is a fair test? | *By using the same volume of soil.* |
| • What could be dangerous in this enquiry? | *The soil might contain germs or animal droppings that could cause illness.* |
| • How could you make sure that you work as safely as possible? | *We need to wear gloves to handle the soil.* |
| • How important will it be to repeat your readings and test each soil more than once? | *It will be very important because it isn't easy to measure some of the volumes very accurately. Also, one type of soil may not be exactly the same all the way through.* |
| • How do we know that different soils have different amounts of air in them? | *We know because when we poured water onto them, the water took up the spaces where the air had been. We found that we could pour more water into some soils than into others, so there must have been more air in some soils than in others.* |
| • How much air do you think there will be in a mixture of two equal amounts of your soils? | *Various answers are possible but children should offer a value between the two values obtained for each soil separately.* |
| • What sort of people might want to know how much air is in different soils? | *Various answers possible, such as gardeners and farmers who grow plants in different soils; architects and builders when they are planning where to build.* |

## Watch out for!

**Safety!** Make sure that children wear plastic gloves to handle soils and that they wash their hands afterwards.

TASK 8

# What is air?

## Purpose

For children to know that air is a mixture of gases.

## What to do

Ask the children to look at the dot picture representing the four main gases in the air. Ask them to talk with each other in pairs or small groups to decide which colour dot represents which gas and to record their decision. Offer an Extra Challenge by asking the children to work out what fraction there is of each gas.

| **QUESTIONS** | ***Possible answers*** |
| --- | --- |
| • Which gas is shown by blue dots? | *Nitrogen –just over three quarters.* |
| • Which is shown by the red dots? | *Oxygen – just under one quarter.* |
| • Which is shown by the yellow dots? | *Argon – a very small amount.* |
| • Which is shown by the green dots? | *Carbon dioxide – a minute amount.* |

## ICT OPPPORTUNITY

Children could use database and graphing software to make a chart from their data.

## Watch out for!

Many children believe that oxygen is the most common gas in the air as oxygen is referred to in everyday life far more than nitrogen. This is because oxygen is a gas that is needed to sustain life; hence its importance to us!

TASK 9

## How heavy is fizz?

### Purpose

For children to know that gases have weight.

### What to do

Provide two cans of fizzy drink per group of children or present this activity as a class demonstration. Follow the steps given in the book, making sure that little or no liquid escapes when the can is opened. Ask the children to think about whether the flat drink will weigh more, the same, or less than the unopened can and to justify their choice. Children are likely to respond in one of three ways:

- The flat drink will weigh more because the light gas bubbles have gone leaving the heavier liquid behind.
- The flat can and the fizzy can will weigh the same because the gas weighs nothing – the mass of liquid is the same in both cans so they will weigh the same.
- The fizzy can will weigh more than the flat can because the fizzy can still has gas in it and gas is real stuff which has mass. As the gas has gone from the flat can it will weigh less than the fizzy can.

This is a good opportunity to instigate a debate. It is important that you do not give them the scientific explanation at this point or indicate what it is. Allow them time to discuss and debate in pairs or small groups, as well as with the whole class.

It is easiest to weigh the cans using digital scales that weigh in grams or tenths of a gram. However, if digital scales are not available then you can compare the masses of the two cans directly using a pan balance. Ask the children to use the evidence to decide which of the above statements is correct.

Remind the children of work they may have already done on writing newspaper reports or take time to discuss the main features of newspaper reports, such as organisation of text using headlines and subheadings, adapting text to fit space, voice and level of formality. Ask them to work in pairs to make notes about the fizzy can experiment using **Task Sheet 5**. Ask them to turn this into a newspaper report that others would want to read.

### ICT OPPORTUNITY

Children could use a word processor or desktop publishing software and a digital camera to produce their report.

### Watch out for!

Children may find it difficult to accept that gas has mass despite the evidence and this may need extra explanation.

TASK 10

# Gas is handy stuff

### Purpose

For children to know that there are many different gases and for them to recognise that gases are important to us because we use them in many different ways.

### What to do

Remind the children about what they said about different gases in Tasks 2 and 3. Point out that we often do not know a lot about gases and their uses and that this is probably because gases are usually invisible. Explain that they will now have a chance to find out as many interesting facts as they can about different gases and their uses. Look at the illustrations of gases being used in everyday life. Find out how many of the questions children can answer before they start their research. They should devise some interesting questions of their own.

Suggest that once they have finished their research each pair should have about four to six interesting questions and answers about gases. Ask them to find a way to get others to look at their questions and answers by making an interactive question and answer board. Look at the examples in the **Pupil's Book** and discuss how they were made.

Once children have finished their question and answer boards, display them and allow time for others to try them out. Ask the children to identify something interesting they have learned from their own or someone else's research.

| QUESTIONS | *Possible answers* |
|---|---|
| • Which gas is used in these balloons? | *Helium.* |
| • Which gases are used in some light bulbs? | *Argon (or xenon).* |
| • Which gas helps to make the foam that firefighters use? | *Carbon dioxide.* |
| • Which gas is put in the tyres of racing cars? | *Nitrogen.* |
| • Which gases are used in hospitals for anaesthetics? | *Nitrous oxide.* |
| • Which gas is put into bags of crisps to stop them getting squashed? | *Nitrogen.* |

### ICT OPPORTUNITY

Children could conduct their research using CD-ROMs or the Internet. Children could improve their database skills and add to the database from Task 3.

TASK 11-12

# Where do gases come from? The perfume particle's journey

**Purpose**

For children to know that gases are formed when liquids evaporate.

**What to do**

For Task 11, set up the water tank and mark the changing water level clearly with the children over a week. Ask them what they think is happening.

This experiment may be worth trying before showing the class to ensure that the level of water decrease is significant enough to measure every day. A warm spot will hasten evaporation and make the effect much more apparent for the children.

For Task 12, put a little perfume on a plate and ask the children to say when they can smell anything. If you ask them to raise their hands as the smell reaches them they should notice that those closest to the perfume smell it first. This indicates that something is travelling outwards from the plate. Next, ask them to think about how the perfume reached their noses. Ask them to make notes about the perfume particle's journey before writing their story. Encourage them to be imaginative and to try to imagine what the perfume particle might say during the different stages of its journey. This activity could also be done as a drama instead of a written story.

| **QUESTIONS** | ***Possible answers*** |
|---|---|
| • The water level went down. Where did the water go? | *Very, very tiny little bits, or particles, of water left the liquid and went into the air.* |
| • If the water went into the air, why am I not getting wet? | *The particles of water are so small that we cannot see or feel them, so they do not make us wet.* |
| • How did the smell of perfume reach my nose? | *The liquid perfume turned into a gas and went into the air. The particles of perfume travelled through the air to the nose.* |
| • Where do gases come from? | *From liquids.* |

**Watch out for!**

Children may realise that gases are also formed when liquids boil. Boiling and evaporation are similar in that gases are formed from liquids, but different in that evaporation takes place over a range of temperatures and at the surface of the liquid whereas boiling takes place at one temperature and throughout the liquid. The important point for children to take on in this particular unit is that gases come from liquids.

TASK 13

# What do gases do?

## Purpose

For children to know that gases do not keep their shape or volume and that gases flow easily, and for them to decide how to answer a question.

## What to do

Ask the children to fill in the table to show what they know about solids and liquids. Point out that they are going to move on to completing the section on gases, but that they are not to do that yet. Now point out that we can not make statements such as 'Liquids change shape', without some evidence to back us up. Ask the children to think how they could find out whether gases change shape or volume and whether they flow easily, using the pictures for ideas. Make sure that equipment such as syringes and balloons are available. Collect together everyone's ideas about the evidence you could present to convince people that gases do not keep their shape or volume but that they flow easily. Ask the children to complete **Task Sheet 6** and then complete their table.

| QUESTIONS | *Possible answers* |
|---|---|
| ◦ How do you know that solids do not flow? | *When you pour them they don't spread out, they form a heap. Each bit of solid stays as it is.* |
| ◦ How do you know that liquids flow? | *When you pour them they spread out and make a level surface.* |
| ◦ How do you know that solids keep their shape? | *If you move a solid from one container to another it doesn't change shape.* |
| ◦ How do you know that liquids do not keep their shape? | *If you move a liquid from one container to another, it changes shape. It takes the shape of its container.* |
| ◦ How do you know that solids do not change volume? | *If you squeeze a solid it still takes up the same amount of space.* |
| ◦ How do you know that liquids do not change volume? | *If you put a liquid in a syringe, block the end, and squeeze it, you can not push the plunger in. The liquid can not be squashed up.* |
| ◦ How could you prove that gases change shape? | *You can partly fill a balloon with some gas (air) and then move it about to change the shape of the balloon and the gas inside.* |
| ◦ How could you prove that gases change volume? | *You can fill a syringe with some gas (air), block the end, and then push in the plunger and squash the gas to change its volume.* |
| ◦ How could you prove that gases flow? | *You can see gas (carbon dioxide) move and flow at pop concerts.* |

## Watch out for!

**Safety!** Always be careful to make sure syringes do not have needles in them and remind the children not to play with them outside school.

TASK 14

# How much gas is in a bottle of pop?

### Purpose

For children to know that gases can be squashed by setting up a fair test and identifying how much to trust their results.

### What to do

Prepare all the equipment and carry out the activity as shown in the **Pupil's Book**. Ask the children to predict how much gas they think will come from a bottle of pop and record their predictions. Set up the equipment, leaving the clip closed, and show the children what will happen to the gas when it escapes from the pop bottle. Do the experiment as a demonstration, using the children to help you. The following method works well:

- Put the beehive stand in the bowl of water.
- Put the tube through the rubber bung.
- Close the clip on the tube.
- Remove the top from the pop bottle and replace quickly with the rubber bung.
- Put the other end of the tube into the beehive stand.
- Invert the measuring cylinder under the surface of the water and rest on the beehive stand.
- Open the clip.
- Gently rock or swirl the bottle to get the gas to come out.
- When the measuring cylinder is full of gas, close the clip.
- Replace with the next measuring cylinder.
- Open the clip.
- Repeat as necessary and continue gently rocking the pop bottle, until all the gas has come out.

You can expect to get about 3 to 4 litres of gas from a 2 litre bottle of pop. Compare the result with the children's predictions. Ask them to consider the questions at the bottom of page 20.

Then ask them to look at the questions on page 21 and to decide how they could answer them. Suggest they choose their question and use **Task Sheet 7** to plan their fair test. Check their plans and let them carry out the test with adult support if needed. When they have finished, ask them to think about how much they can trust their results, recording their results on **Task Sheet 8**.

| QUESTIONS | ***Possible answers*** |
|---|---|
| ◦ Was the gas in the pop bottle squeezed up? How do you know? | *The gas was squeezed up because when we let the gas out of the pop bottle, it took up lots more space.* |
| ◦ Why do you think we often burp after drinking pop? | *We burp because the gas in the fizzy drink is squashed up. When it gets inside us it spreads out and bubbles up as a burp.* |
| ◦ Do you think we got all the gas out? | *It was difficult to tell because at the end the gas was only coming out very slowly. We might have stopped before it all came out.* |
| ◦ Did any of the gas escape? | *It may have escaped when we put in the rubber bung and whenever we opened and closed the clip.* |

## CHECKPOINT 2 Helping your pen-friend

Children are asked to write to a pen-friend with their suggestions on some statements about gases. Ask them to look at the text and to write comments on it using **Task Sheet 9**.

Encourage the children to look back at their original ideas about gases and the questions they asked in Tasks 2 and 3, and to say what they have learned and how their ideas have changed.

## S Summary

An opportunity for the children to assess their own progress using the **Science Log**. Tell the children to circle the face that best reflects how confident they are with each statement.

## A Assessment Tasks

An assessment of children's learning. Give the children **Assessment Task Sheets A** and **B**. The questions are below, with selected answers in *italics*.

### ANSWERS

**1** Jo looked at a jar containing sand. She said, "There is nothing but sand in here." Explain why she is wrong. *There is also air in the jar with the sand.*

**2** A gardener wanted to find out how much air was in his soil. He poured water onto some soil to replace the air. He saw how much water he could pour into the soil.
He then repeated his reading twice. Why did he do this?
*To get a more accurate reading and make sure that the first reading wasn't a mistake.*

**3** Draw a line to match each gas to its use.

| | |
|---|---|
| helium | Is put inside light bulbs. |
| argon | Is needed for us to live. |
| carbon dioxide | Is put into lighter-than-air balloons. |
| oxygen | Is put into fizzy drinks. |

**4** Four of the statements below are true. Tick those you think are true.

| | |
|---|---|
| All gases are smelly. | |
| All gases can change shape. | ✔ |
| All gases can flow. | ✔ |
| All gases explode near a lighted match. | |
| All gases can change volume. | ✔ |
| All gases are invisible. | |
| All gases have mass. | ✔ |

## B

**1** "Evaporation is when a solid turns into a liquid," said Anna. Explain to her that she is wrong. How can you record evaporation?
*Evaporation is when a liquid turns into a gas. When a solid turns into a liquid this is called melting.*

**2** Tick which of these would evaporate at room temperature.

| Material | Will it evaporate? |
|---|---|
| Water | ✔ |
| Metal | |
| Wax | |
| Perfume | ✔ |
| A sponge | |

**3** Why are these statements incorrect?

- Air is made of two types of gas. *Air is made of many different gases.*
- Oxygen isn't useful for us to breathe. *We must breathe oxygen to live.*
- Carbon dioxide is the only useful gas. *Oxygen is certainly useful, as are argon and helium for commercial uses.*
- Soil and gravel don't contain any air. *There is air in between the solid particles.*

# Task Sheet 1

*Name* ............................................ *Date* ............................

What ...

Why ...

How ...

Which ...

Where ...



**New Star Science** Ginn and Company 2001
Copying permitted for purchasing school only. This material is not copyright free.

# Task Sheet 2

*Name* ..................................................... *Date* .....................................

Copying permitted for purchasing school only. This material is not copyright free.

# Task Sheet 3

*Name* ........................................ *Date* ........................................

**We will change:**

______________________________________________________________

**We will measure:**

______________________________________________________________

**We will keep these things the same:**

______________________________________________________________

______________________________________________________________

**This is what we need to do to make sure we do this scientific enquiry as safely as possible:**

______________________________________________________________

______________________________________________________________

**It is important to take repeat readings when we do this enquiry because:**

______________________________________________________________

______________________________________________________________



**New Star Science** Ginn and Company 2001
Copying permitted for purchasing school only. This material is not copyright free.

# Task Sheet 4

*Name* ..........................................  *Date* ..........................

| **Type of soil** | **How much air?** | | | |
|---|---|---|---|---|
| | **1st go** | **2nd go** | **3rd go** | **Middle reading** |
| | | | | |
| | | | | |
| | | | | |

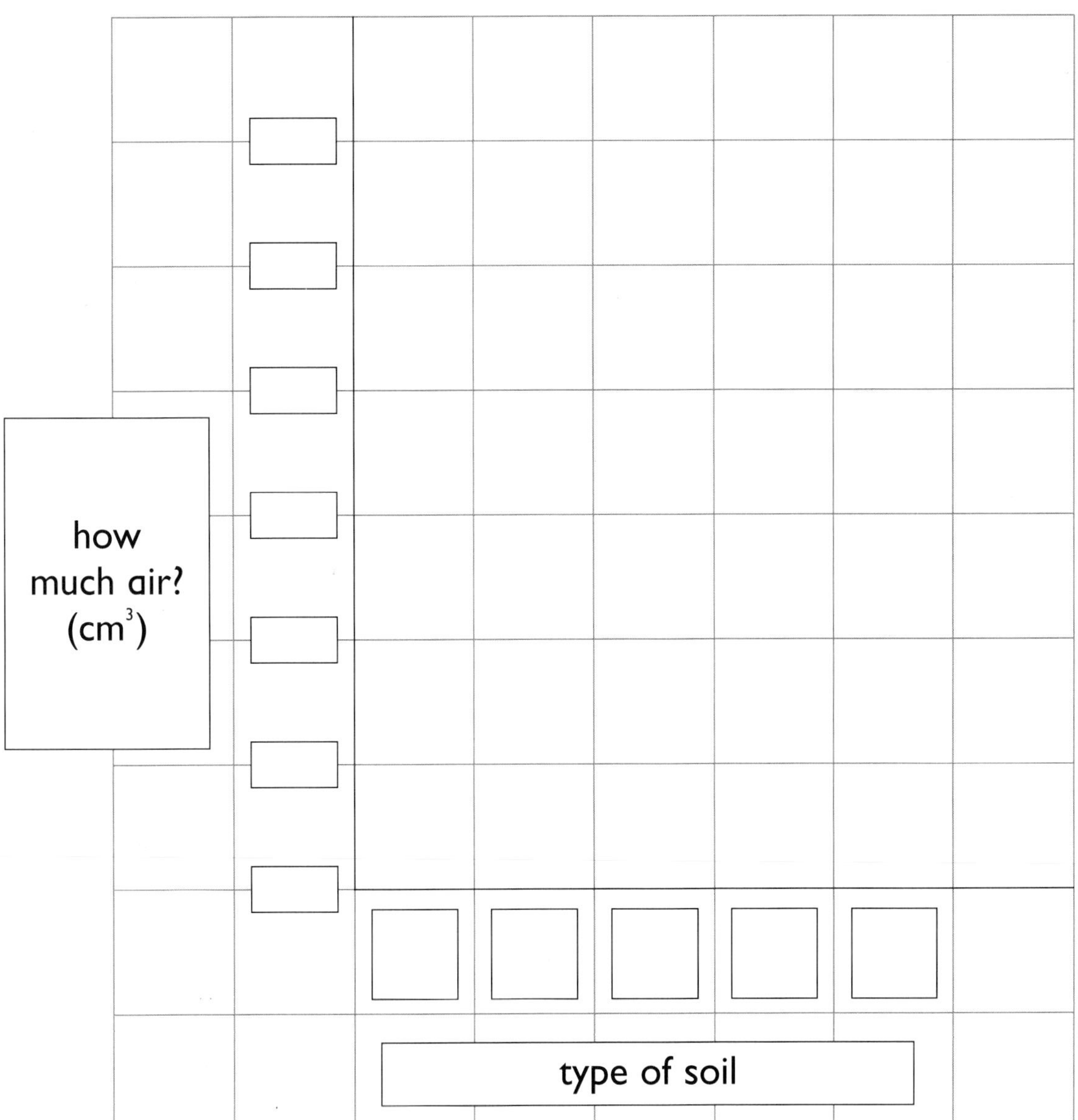



Copying permitted for purchasing school only. This material is not copyright free.

# Task Sheet 5

*Name* ............................................................ *Date* ..............................

Who was doing the experiment?

______________________________________________

Why were they doing it?

______________________________________________

What did they do?

______________________________________________

What did they find out?

______________________________________________

Was it surprising? Why?

______________________________________________

**Possible quotes for the report:**

| Name | What they said |
|---|---|
| | |
| | |
| | |

A good headline:

______________________________________________



**New Star Science** Ginn and Company 2001
Copying permitted for purchasing school only. This material is not copyright free.

# Task Sheet 6

*Name* ........................................ *Date* ....................

Gases do not keep their shape. What is your evidence for this?

Gases do not keep their volume. What is your evidence for this?

Gases flow easily. What is your evidence for this?

**New Star Science** Ginn and Company 2001
Copying permitted for purchasing school only. This material is not copyright free.

# Task Sheet 7

*Name* ........................................ *Date* ....................

**Our question:**

______________________________________________

**We will change:**

______________________________________________

**We will measure:**

______________________________________________

**We will keep these things the same:**

______________________________________________

**This is a picture of the equipment we are going to use:**

**These parts of our scientific enquiry might be tricky to do:**

______________________________________________

______________________________________________



**New Star Science** Ginn and Company 2001
Copying permitted for purchasing school only. This material is not copyright free.

# Task Sheet 8

*Name* ..............................  *Date* ..............................

| | |
|---|---|
| | |
| | |
| | |
| | |
| | |

We found that:

______________________________

______________________________

______________________________

During the enquiry gas may have escaped when:

______________________________

______________________________

______________________________

We are not sure that all the gas came out of the pop bottle because:

______________________________

______________________________

______________________________

How accurate do you think your results are? Circle one answer.

Very accurate    Quite accurate    Not very accurate    Not at all accurate

How much can you trust your results? Circle one answer.

Complete trust    Some trust    A little trust    No trust

**New Star Science** Ginn and Company 2001
Copying permitted for purchasing school only. This material is not copyright free.

# Task Sheet 9

*Name* ..................................................... *Date* ..................................

Information about gases:

1. There are lots of different gases.
2. Air is made of one type of gas.
3. Air gets everywhere; it is even in the soil.
4. Other than air, gases are not useful.
5. Most other gases are smelly and dangerous.
6. When liquids evaporate gases are formed.
7. Gases behave like liquids. They do not keep their shape; they flow; they keep their volume.

Air is a mixture of gases. It is not just one gas.



**New Star Science** Ginn and Company 2001
Copying permitted for purchasing school only. This material is not copyright free.

# Science Log

*Name* ..........................................................  *Date* ..........................................

- I know that there are differences between solids and liquids.
- I know that air has weight and is all around us.
- I can show that air is a real material.
- I know that solid materials have air in the 'gaps'.
- I know that soils have air trapped in them.
- I know when to repeat measurements.
- I know that gases have weight.
- I know that there are many gases and many of these are important to us.
- I know that gases are formed when liquids evaporate.
- I know that gases do not keep their shape or volume.
- I know that gases flow easily.
- I can identify differences between solids, liquids and gases.

**New Star Science** Ginn and Company 2001
Copying permitted for purchasing school only. This material is not copyright free.

# Assessment Task Sheet A

*Name* ............................................................ *Date* ....................................

**1** Jo looked at a jar containing sand. She said, " There is nothing but sand in here." Explain why she is wrong.

______________________________________________

**2** A gardener wanted to find out how much air was in his soil. He poured water onto some soil to replace the air. He saw how much water he could pour into the soil. He then repeated his reading twice. Why did he do this?

______________________________________________

______________________________________________

______________________________________________

**3** Draw a line to match each gas to its use.

| | |
|---|---|
| helium | Is put inside light bulbs. |
| argon | Is needed for us to live. |
| carbon dioxide | Is put into lighter-than-air balloons. |
| oxygen | Is put into fizzy drinks. |

**4** Four of the statements below are true. Tick those you think are true.

All gases are smelly.

All gases can change shape.

All gases can flow.

All gases explode near a lighted match.

All gases can change volume.

All gases are invisible.

All gases have weight.



**New Star Science** Ginn and Company 2001
Copying permitted for purchasing school only. This material is not copyright free.

# Assessment Task Sheet B

*Name* ..............................  *Date* ..............................

**1** " Evaporation is when a solid turns into a liquid," said Anna. Explain to her that she is wrong.

______________________________

______________________________

______________________________

**2** Tick which of these would evaporate at room temperature.

| **Material** | **Will it evaporate?** |
|---|---|
| Water | |
| Metal | |
| Wax | |
| Perfume | |
| A sponge | |

**3** Why are these statements incorrect?

- Air is made of two types of gas.

______________________________

- Oxygen isn't useful for us to breathe.

______________________________

- Carbon dioxide is the only useful gas.

______________________________

- Soil and gravel don't contain any air.

______________________________


Copying permitted for purchasing school only. This material is not copyright free.

# Curriculum Links

## England National Curriculum

Sc1 Scientific enquiry – *all*

Sc3 Materials and their properties:

*Grouping and classifying materials – 1e*

*Changing materials – 2d, 2g*

*Separating mixtures of materials – 3e*

## Northern Ireland Curriculum

Key Stage 2

Investigating and making in Science and Technology – *all*

Materials:

*Properties – d*

*Change – e*

## Environmental Studies 5-14 in Scottish schools

Earth and Space:

*Materials from Earth – levels C, E*

*Changing Materials – levels B, C*

Skills in Science: Investigating – *all*

## Wales National Curriculum

Key Stage 2

Scientific Enquiry – *all*

Materials and their Properties:

*Grouping and Classifying Materials – 5*



**New Star Science** Ginn and Company 2001
Copying permitted for purchasing school only. This material is not copyright free.

# NEW STAR SCIENCE SKILLS LADDER

| | Planning | | | | | Obtaining and presenting evidence | | | Considering evidence and evaluating | | | |
|---|---|---|---|---|---|---|---|---|---|---|---|---|
| | **Asking questions and having ideas** | **Deciding an appropriate approach** | **Planning the detail of what to do** | **Predicting what might happen** | **Choosing what equipment to use** | **Using equipment and carrying out practical work safely** | **Making observations and taking measurements** | **Presenting evidence** | **Drawing conclusions and describing patterns and trends** | **Comparing results to predictions and making further predictions** | **Explaining evidence** | **Evaluating** |
| **Year 4** | Asks questions and offers own ideas for scientific enquiry. | With support knows when to answer a question by using a fair test and when evidence should be collected in other ways. | In a fair test, identifies what to keep the same and with support what to change and what to measure/observe. Plans main steps in other enquiries. Recognises hazards and, with support, plans how to control risks. | Predicts outcomes and sometimes suggests reasons for their prediction. | Selects appropriate equipment and with support, considers the scale and the degree of accuracy required on some measuring equipment. | Uses basic equipment correctly and safely. Begins to deal with equipment failures. | Makes a series of observations. Uses standard measuring equipment for measuring most quantities. | Creates own tables and bar charts. Uses a line chart with support. | Makes a general statement about simple patterns in results. | Makes further predictions from results in simple contexts. | Provides explanations for simple patterns in results. | Suggests how the enquiry might be improved. With support, recognises some of the limitations of their evidence. |
| **Year 5** | Asks questions and offers own ideas for scientific enquiry and, with support, improves question to clarify scientific purpose. | Knows when to answer a question by using a fair test and when evidence should be collected in other ways, including using secondary sources. | Sets up a fair test knowing what to change, what to measure/observe and what to keep the same. With support, considers whether to take repeat readings With support, plans the detail in other types of enquiry. Assesses hazards and plans how to control risks. | Predicts outcomes and, where appropriate, suggests reasons for their predictions. | Selects equipment from a wider range, including digital scales, forcemeters and computer sensors. With support, considers the scale and the degree of accuracy required on measuring equipment. | Uses a wide range of equipment correctly and safely. Deals with most equipment failures independently. | Makes a series of relevant observations. With support, takes accurate readings on measuring equipment, repeating them where necessary. | Begins to select appropriate way to present evidence. Creates own bar charts and tables, including those for repeat readings Creates a line graph with support. | With support, describes relationships identified, linking both factors and describing whole relationship in comparative terms. | With support, makes further predictions from results and uses these to test out the suggested pattern in the relationship studied. | Sometimes relates patterns in results to scientific knowledge where appropriate. | Identifies how much to trust results. Suggests reasons why similar enquiries yield different results. With support, considers the spread of repeated measurements. With support, recognises some of the limitations of their evidence. |
| **Year 6** | Asks questions and offers own ideas for scientific enquiry which have a clear scientific purpose. | Identifies appropriate approach to answer a scientific question. | Sets up a fair test. Plans the detail in other types of enquiry. Decides whether to take repeat readings. With support, considers whether plans will yield enough evidence for the task. Assesses hazards and plans how to control risks. | Predicts outcomes and, where appropriate, sketches a graph to show the expected pattern in results. Justifies their predictions using scientific knowledge when possible. | Selects suitable equipment for a range of tasks. Takes into account the scale and the degree of accuracy required on measuring equipment. | Uses a wide range of equipment correctly and safely. Deals with equipment failures independently. | Makes a series of relevant observations. Takes accurate readings on measuring equipment, repeating them where necessary. | Selects suitable way to present evidence. Where appropriate, draws up line graph independently, except where scales involve very large or very small numbers. | Describes relationships identified, linking both factors and describing whole relationship in comparative terms. | Makes further predictions from results and uses these to test out the suggested pattern in the relationship studied. | Relates patterns in results to scientific knowledge where appropriate. | Identifies how much to trust results and justifies decision. Suggests reasons why similar enquiries yield different results. Considers the spread of repeated measurements. Recognises some of the limitations of their evidence. |